MEDITATIONS FOR MODERN MAN

or Wisdom from your Father

Michael William Cook

Cook Publications

Copyright © 2021 Michael William Cook

All rights reserved

The characters and events portrayed in this book are fictitious. Any similarity to real persons, living or dead, is coincidental and not intended by the author.

No part of this book may be reproduced, or stored in a retrieval system, or transmitted in any form or by any means, electronic, mechanical, photocopying, recording, or otherwise, without express written permission of the publisher.

ISBN-13: 9798548793140

Cover design by: Art Painter
Cover photograph by: Michael William Cook
Library of Congress Control Number: 2018675309
Printed in the United States of America

*To all the sons and daughters who long for
the wisdom of their parents.*

"The special mark of the modern world is not that it is skeptical, but that it is dogmatic without knowing it. It says, in mockery of the old devotees, that they believed without knowing why they believed. But the moderns believe without knowing what they believe – and without even knowing that they do believe it... Their thoughts will work out to the most interesting conclusions, but they can never tell you anything about their beginnings. They have always taken away the number they first thought of. They have always forgotten the very fact or fancy on which their whole theory depends."

— G.K. CHESTERTON, WRITER

CONTENTS

Title Page
Copyright
Dedication
Epigraph
Trigger Warning
Introduction
Preface
Logical Fallacies

1. Leadership	1
2. Morality	16
3. Logic	33
4. Facts	50
5. Liberty	70
6. Criticism	91
7. Character	108
8. Education	130
9. Politics	142
About The Author	155

TRIGGER WARNING

This book contains content that could be emotionally and intellectually challenging to the reader. If you are easily offended by well-reasoned opinions, you may be triggered. If you cannot accept everyone does not agree with your beliefs, you may be triggered. If you are intolerant of exploring alternate viewpoints, you may be triggered. If you cannot logically justify your accepted dogma, you may be triggered. If your behavior is ruled by your emotions, you may be triggered. If you are easily triggered, this book provides the opportunity to challenge your strongly held beliefs and question your cultural conditioning. An open mind is a free mind. Recent studies *"suggest a trigger warning is neither meaningfully helpful nor harmful."*[1]

---

1. Sanson M, Strange D, Garry M. Trigger Warnings Are Trivially Helpful at Reducing Negative Affect, Intrusive Thoughts, and Avoidance. Clinical Psychological Science. 2019;7(4):778-793. doi:10.1177/2167702619827018

INTRODUCTION

As a history enthusiast, I tend to frame events and ideas in a historical context. For instance, when Emperor Marcus Aurelius Antonius (reigned 161-180 AD) wrote his 12 books of Meditations the Roman Empire was at its zenith. Marcus is known as a wise and noble emperor - the epitome of Aristotle's Philosopher King. Based upon the Greek Stoic Philosophy, Marcus wrote for his mental stimulation and self-improvement. Although these were personal writings not intend for public consumption, I suspect his intended audience was his son and heir to the throne - Emperor Commodus.

Much like a student, children do not always appreciate the wisdom of their elders. Few children follow their parent's advice and are determined to learn life lessons the hard way. Unfortunately, some children will never understand the Maxims. But ultimately a child learns to value truthful wisdom based upon the parent's life experiences.

Anyone who has lost a parent, grandparent, or other mentor regrets not asking certain questions or worse struggles to recall the answer. Some mistakenly believe these truths or Maxims are not relevant. The truth is often debated but always relevant.

No one should be censored, demeaned, or shunned because the truth makes someone else feel uncomfortable. No one can control how another person feels. Everyone is responsible for his or her behavior regardless of the human tendency to project blame onto others while avoiding responsibility for themselves.

President John Adams (in office 1797-1801) once said,

"*Facts are stubborn things; and whatever may be our wishes, our inclinations, or the dictates of our passion, they cannot alter the state of facts and evidence.*" He said this in 1770 as the lawyer defending the British soldiers who fired upon a group of 50 Colonists at what was later called the Boston Massacre.

Due to the heightened emotion, most Colonists prejudged the soldiers guilty of murder. However, Adams proved to the jury that the soldiers were provoked by the crowd before the shooting. The jury acquitted Captain Preston due to "*reasonable doubt*". Adams successfully argued that the facts outweigh the emotion. He was most likely quoting a proverb but his "*Facts are stubborn things*" Maxim still resonates.

PREFACE

This book, "*Meditations for Modern Man*" is broken up into nine chapters: Leadership, Morality, Logic, Facts, Liberty, Criticism, Character, Education, and Politics. Each section starts with a definition and proceeds with Maxims I developed by being a loyal follower, moral leader, and compassionate parent.

Because many of my Maxims are derived from exposing a failure in Logic, the most common informal fallacies that can arise during a discussion or debate are in the preface. For further information, search for *"Principles of Logic"* on the Internet to learn about Logical Arguments, Syllogisms, Fallacies, Square of Opposition, and Venn Diagrams.

If this piques your interest I highly recommend enrolling in an Introductory to Philosophy or Principles of Logic class. Alternatively, you can watch YouTube videos or listen to Podcasts that dive deep into Philosophy and Logic. Although it is not necessary, a rudimentary foundation in Logical Reasoning knowledge can help the reader understand the underpinnings of most Maxims.

LOGICAL FALLACIES

Ad Hominem. Attacking the person proposing the argument instead of the argument.

Appeal to Authority. Concluding an argument is true because a person in authority asserts it.

Appeal to Emotion. Using emotions such as fear, pity, and flattery to persuade instead of sound reason.

Appeal to Hypocrisy. Disregarding an argument because the opponent fails to act per that position.

Appeal to Motive. Dismissing a conclusion by questioning the motive of the person proposing the argument.

Appeal to Tradition. Concluding an argument is true because it has longevity.

Argument from Silence. Reaching a conclusion based on the silence or lack of contrary evidence.

Argumentum Ad Populum. Concluding an argument is true simply because lots of people agree.

Begging the Question. Conclusion of an argument is assumed in one of the premises (a.k.a. circular reasoning).

Cherry Picking. Only using data confirming a particular argument while ignoring data contradicting it.

False Dilemma. Holding only two possible conclusions as options when there are other valid options.

Post Hoc Ergo Propter Hoc. Reaching a conclusion of causation because one event followed another event.

Red Herring. Changing the subject to divert attention from the original argument being proposed.

Slippery Slope. Asserts that a relatively small step will lead to a chain of events resulting in a drastic conclusion.

Strawman. Misrepresentation of an opponent's argument which is attacked instead of the original argument.

1. LEADERSHIP

Leadership is the office or position of a leader (a person who directs a military force or unit with commanding authority or influence) and the capacity to lead.

Leadership is finding what people are capable of doing, even when that person does not yet know they can.

* * *

If a task is managed by many people, things are missed because there is no single leader.

* * *

Most people are not leaders because they want plausible deniability for all decisions made that affect their lives. These people are sheep who only know how to begrudgingly follow.

* * *

A timely 80% solution is always better than a tardy 100% solution.

* * *

The first to lead is not always the best to lead.

* * *

Desiring a Leadership position is not equal to having a Leadership ability.

* * *

There is no excuse for lack of planning.

✻ ✻ ✻

Never fail due to lack of effort but rather let lack of ability be the culprit.

* * *

Let failure be the domain of lack of skill or ability not lack of planning and leadership.

* * *

If everyone is leading, no one is leading. At best a committee can merely manage and is a caretaker of events.

❋ ❋ ❋

If no one is behind you,
you are not leading.

* * *

If you do not care where you are going you do not need a compass nor a map. Enjoy the uncharted voyage.

❈ ❈ ❈

Life does not have subtitles nor a rewind button, so pay attention the first time.

* * *

When assigned a task, chore, project, or any job there is one inescapable truth: the longer you take, the longer it takes.

2. MORALITY

Morality is a doctrine expressing a concept of right behavior, conformity to ideals of right human conduct, and sanctioned by one's conscience or ethical judgment.

Unless an order (or law) is illegal, immoral, or unethical; one must follow it but one does not have to like it.

❊ ❊ ❊

If you treat an adult like a child, the adult will continue to act like a child.

* * *

Never condone immorality because it is never permissible by a moral person.

✻ ✻ ✻

Treat other people with respect and dignity until they prove unworthy of respect; however, dignity is the right of all people.

❉ ❉ ❉

If accomplishing a difficult goal was easy, more people would accomplish it.

❋ ❋ ❋

Sometimes doing nothing is the best decision, especially following a crisis.

* * *

The best decisions take time to percolate devoid of emotional reactionism.

❉ ❉ ❉

Every action is a choice, even if you choose to not act.

* * *

A racist sees racism everywhere much as a good person sees good people everywhere.

❋ ❋ ❋

The best revenge is to be happy in life and successful. Happiness loves company more than misery needs company.

❋ ❋ ❋

Just because other people change, it does not mean you have to change.

❋ ❋ ❋

Prayers are not pity but the request that God gives his blessings to those most in need of His grace, mercy, and intercession.

❊ ❊ ❊

Poverty does not make a person noble anymore than wealth makes a person evil. Actions, not incomes, define people as noble or evil.

* * *

An Evil man doing a good deed does not make him a good man any more than a Good man doing a bad deed makes him an Evil man. In both instances, his heart stays the same.

❋ ❋ ❋

Be mindful of people who desire death and destruction on others with whom they disagree during a crisis; the person's true self is unmasked to reveal an Evil heart.

❋ ❋ ❋

A good parent is not a minor child's friend but a successful parent has raised an adult worthy of friendship.

3. LOGIC

Logic is a science that deals with the principles and criteria of validity of inference and demonstration and a particular mode of reasoning viewed as valid or faulty.

Those who cannot win a logical argument tend to change the definitions of words to steal the argument.

❈ ❈ ❈

Much like a carpenter cutting lumber; think twice but act once.

❊ ❊ ❊

An emotional mind is blind to reason, quick to anger, and intolerant of contrary thoughts.

❋ ❋ ❋

Trying repeatedly to convince an ignorant person of his or her faulty logic makes one potentially insane to expect a different result. Use the rule of three then leave the ignorant be.

❊ ❊ ❊

Appeals to Emotion are the telltale sign the person advocating an action (or inaction) cannot logically defend that action (or inaction).

❊ ❊ ❊

An opinion or logical argument that is not challenged is not defended. Untested opinions are not valid opinions.

❋ ❋ ❋

When Logic fails,
Emotion reigns.

* * *

Self-proclaimed liberals redefine well-established words, then attack that definition in a new argument identified as a Strawman Fallacy.

* * *

If people are reacting emotionally, they are not thinking critically.

* * *

The desire to criminalizing contrary opinions, especially political opinions, is the telltale sign the person advocating an opinion cannot withstand rational scrutiny.

✻ ✻ ✻

Everyone can equally have an opinion but everyone's opinion is not equal.

* * *

Studying a contrary argument can confirm your initial position or it can help you refine your position which is more beneficial.

❊ ❊ ❊

If people do not like the logical argument, people tend to solely attack the messenger rather than contemplate the legitimacy of the argument itself.

※ ※ ※

The Ad Hominem logical fallacy of attacking the messenger provides a false sense of empowerment when the reality is utter impotence of the accuser.

❊ ❊ ❊

Redefine the terms or definitions to control the narrative and steal the logical argument is disingenuous at best and deceitful at worse.

❊ ❊ ❊

When actions are based primarily on fear and feelings, actions cannot be logically explained or adequately exculpated.

4. FACTS

Facts are things that have an actual existence, an actual occurrence, and a piece of information presented as having objective reality.

In the absence of facts, the human mind speculates.

✻ ✻ ✻

An old lie is still a lie. A falsehood's longevity does not legitimize it.

❋ ❋ ❋

A strongly held belief does not beget a fact, however, facts are the bedrock of a rationally held belief.

✻ ✻ ✻

Facts exist independently of a person's feelings.

✽ ✽ ✽

Feelings do not trump facts any more than the Moon outshines the Sun.

✻ ✻ ✻

If science was a settled fact, then science would not be redefined so often.

* * *

Do not form an opinion of someone else based on the heresy of others but rather base your opinion on documented facts and personal observations.

❊ ❊ ❊

The truth is always relevant and facts are always pertinent.

✽ ✽ ✽

If you are going to be
wrong; at least
be consistent.

❊ ❊ ❊

Most people do not create things, instead, most people re-create things.

* * *

A good bottle of Scotch is always appreciated whereas a poor quality of Scotch insults both the giver and receiver.

❋ ❋ ❋

It is a waste of time and effort to discuss topics with someone who is intellectually dishonest.

✻ ✻ ✻

If a rising tide elevates all vessels then a sinking ship drowns all aboard.

✻ ✻ ✻

A virus does not care if you are good or bad, pretty or plain, fat or thin, tall or short, rich or poor, employed or jobless, partisan or agnostic, a science supporter or a science denier; a virus is an equal opportunity destroyer of man.

* * *

Eating another person's cake doesn't make it your birthday.

✣ ✣ ✣

Truthfulness occurs when people are afraid you see them for what they really are.

* * *

Fear exposes the polite veneer to reveal a person's underlying true values, principles, views, and beliefs.

❋ ❋ ❋

A scared person is a more honest person.

❋ ❋ ❋

Those who are not in control of their own emotions and feelings inevitably blame others for how they personally feel.

5. LIBERTY

Liberty is the state of being free, freedom from physical restraint, freedom from despotic control, and the power of choice.

The most powerful word a free person can say is "No".

* * *

Nothing is ever free, it must be paid for in exchange of individual responsibility and personal liberty.

* * *

Government funds for goods and services come with an exchange of personal choice and individual freedom.

※ ※ ※

Pay your own way and retain freedom of choice.

* * *

Freedom is correlated to responsibility: more freedom demands more responsibility.

❋ ❋ ❋

The only way to defeat a National Populist candidate is to destroy a Nation's founding, heroes, history, values, traditions, institutions, freedoms, economy, and success.

✺ ✺ ✺

When blind compliance is compulsory, freedom is dead.

❄ ❄ ❄

Everyone has an opportunity in the United States, only the quantity of opportunities differ.

※ ※ ※

If a person is homeless in the United States, it is a result of multiple bad choices made by that individual.

❋ ❋ ❋

People ignorant of history are quick to state a current event is the best or worse event in history especially when discussing Liberty and Freedom.

❊ ❊ ❊

Opportunity is like the branches of a tree, each branch removed decreases blossoms until there remains one trunk from the roots in the ground to a single branch in the sky.

✻ ✻ ✻

Never limit yourself to the possible but rather attempt to achieve the improbable.

* * *

You cannot learn from the successes or mistakes of History unless you are humble enough to realize you are no better than those who came before you.

❋ ❋ ❋

Opportunity is bringing someone to a doorway, the person must walk through it of their own volition.

❊ ❊ ❊

Success must have the potential to fail to be meaningful.

❋ ❋ ❋

Institutional Entitlement is a disease without a cure.

❋ ❋ ❋

Blind compliance is the motto of a despotic government.

✻ ✻ ✻

Traditional American independence and self-reliance are quickly devolving into American dependence and self-indulgence.

❊ ❊ ❊

A rule that permits exceptions does not justify creating a new rule for the exceptions.

✻ ✻ ✻

People in need demand more government, whereas people with means demand less government.

6. CRITICISM

Criticism is the act of criticizing usually unfavorably, a critic (one with a reasoned opinion on any matter involving a judgment) who expresses an observation or remark.

The Cult of Political Correctness practices intolerance, outrage, and censorship to silence its critics by holding others to a standard it cannot achieve itself.

※ ※ ※

Anytime someone says a situation is complicated it is really a simple situation that is undesired.

✻ ✻ ✻

If you never stray from the basics, you never have to go back to basics.

❊ ❊ ❊

You choose your attitude, no one can choose it for you.

❈ ❈ ❈

There are two types of people in this world: you either have a pair of balls or you cling to a pair.

❈ ❈ ❈

The most intolerant people in this world are those people who demand tolerance from everyone else.

❋ ❋ ❋

People have formed who they are as a person by 18 to 25 years old. After that, barring a traumatic event, no one really changes.

❊ ❊ ❊

If you demand respect from others, respect all others - not just those with whom you agree.

✻ ✻ ✻

Taxing other people (but not yourself) to pay for unearned programs for the poor does not make you a charitable person, it makes you a thief and a hypocrite.

❊ ❊ ❊

When hearing criticism ask yourself three questions: "Is this true?", "Does changing improve it?", and "Do I want to change?"

* * *

All advice, criticism, and suggestions must be scrutinized initially by considering the source.

❊ ❊ ❊

When criticized consider the source and ask if true before you contemplate improvement. Otherwise, dismiss it and move on.

❉ ❉ ❉

Criticism does not elevate the critic but only has the potential to elevate the object of the criticism.

❊ ❊ ❊

Accusations fueled by unnamed sources are the worse form of character assassination by the most cowardly of foes.

✻ ✻ ✻

Outrageous allegations without proof speak more to the character of the accuser than that of the accused.

✺ ✺ ✺

It takes a generation to validate successful parenting and another generation for the children to admit or understand successful parenting.

7. CHARACTER

Character is moral excellence; an attribute that distinguishes a person; and a complex of mental and ethical traits marking an individual, group, or nation.

We are the sum of our own actions and inactions.

* * *

Policies and people, practices and procedures always change; therefore do what you know is right... which does not change.

※ ※ ※

No matter what event occurs, you are the master of your own behavior.

❋ ❋ ❋

If you half-ass something you will end up doing it again. If you full-ass something you will only do it once.

❋ ❋ ❋

Reserve the final judgment of others to God, however, exercise temporal judgment for yourself.

✸ ✸ ✸

Never demand another person act in a manner in which you do not act.

❋ ❋ ❋

Liars, hypocrites, and thieves are the Evil trinity of vices.

* * *

Mutual respect in our modern society is a lost social grace.

❋ ❋ ❋

Honesty and integrity never go out of style.

* * *

Trust in God but in all else verify and triple check because Prudence is a virtue.

* * *

Everyone at some point will fail. How one responds to failure is the definition of one's character.

※ ※ ※

Anything is easy once you know how to do it.

✸ ✸ ✸

You can always tell
the sins of your enemy
by the accusations your
enemy project onto you.

※ ※ ※

If you cannot be nice, be quiet; conversely, if you cannot be quiet, be nice.

❊ ❊ ❊

In everything we do in life, the least someone can do is be prompt. Being on time is an ability within anyone's grasp.

※ ※ ※

Excelling at something you enjoy is easier than excelling at something you dislike, however, successful people excel at both.

* * *

Doing what is right at the right time is never outdated it merely falls out of fashion.

❋ ❋ ❋

In difficult situations, it is human instinct to withdraw but it is selfless courage to remain steadfast.

* * *

Having a larger number of people agree with you does not make you right, just as having a large number of people disagree with you does not make you wrong.

* * *

The tallest tree stands alone.

* * *

Never underestimate a good sense of humor; it is the elixir of a healthy life.

8. EDUCATION

Education is the process of being educated (giving evidence of training or practice), the resulting knowledge and development, and methods of learning in schools.

Education is the great
social equalizer
of mankind.

* * *

Real intelligence (not to be confused with education) is performing well in studies in which you are not interested.

✣ ✣ ✣

An educated man who does not possess a trade skill is a deficient man NOT a smarter man.

❋ ❋ ❋

Education is the great equalizer among the classes, whereas the ability to APPLY that knowledge makes you superior to your fellow students.

❊ ❊ ❊

Those who can do things for themselves are not beholden to the time, talent, and treasure of others.

❋ ❋ ❋

Successfully "adulting" in the 21st Century requires effort and knowledge. If you are lacking in one you require more of the other.

❋ ❋ ❋

Life Skills are severely underappreciated but greatly needed.

❋ ❋ ❋

Basic tradecraft - carpentry, electricity, plumbing, painting - are skills useful in life.

* * *

Learning a trade like carpentry, painting, plumbing, electrician, etc. will increase your individual Liberty and personal satisfaction.

* * *

In life, giving 100% effort is better than scoring 100% grade.

* * *

If you make no mistakes, you learn little and miss opportunities for improvement.

9. POLITICS

Politics is the science concerned with influencing governmental policy, competition between groups vying for power, and the relations between people living in society.

Perpetual fear is the key
to a successful revolution.

✳ ✳ ✳

Tyrants keep the masses compliant by using fear to control them.

✳ ✳ ✳

Fear begets honesty. Prefer to know what people actually think, not what those people want you to believe they think.

❊ ❊ ❊

Organized religions do not have a monopoly on blind faith, intellectual dishonesty, irrational arguments, and religious zeal. The irrational Political Zealots are far more dangerous.

* * *

Most people who claim to be "Independent" vote in Democrat Primaries, caucus with Democrats, support Democrat policies, and vote for Democrat candidates. This is not a political independent but rather a dogmatic person who cannot defend his or her choices and wants to be inoculated from the result.

❈ ❈ ❈

Self-proclaimed liberals never see their own hypocrisy because they feel justified in their strongly held beliefs.

❊ ❊ ❊

Self-proclaimed liberals feel entitled to control the Judicial Branch much like the media, science, education, and Hollywood controls their specific domain. Anyone who deviates from the liberal dogma of each domain is persecuted by the self-appointed fact-checkers.

* * *

You cannot quell the perpetual outrage culture because capitulation emboldens radicals to reach beyond their grasp.

❊ ❊ ❊

Never underestimate the ability of woke people to effortlessly divine an offense from the benign.

* * *

Fear has to be continuously fed with emotional appeals or it dissipates when dire predictions and false outrage fall flat from careful reason.

* * *

The perpetually offended are also the perpetually unhappy.

❋ ❋ ❋

To fail is human, to blame your brother for your own failure is fratricide.

ABOUT THE AUTHOR

Michael William Cook

Michael William Cook, a retired Major from the United States Air Force (USAF), earned a Bachelor of Science from the University of Maryland and a Masters of Business Administration from the University of Phoenix. He led Airmen in the USAF, guided Scouts in the Boy Scouts of America, and raised four children with his wife. He graduated from four Air Force leadership schools and served on three continents as an Enlisted Airman, a Non-Commissioned Officer, and a Commissioned Officer. The preceding wisdom is maxims he developed as a follower, leader, and parent. Michael is also the author of "Passamaquoddy Legends (Annotated Edition)" available exclusively on Amazon. He is currently working on an original book of poems and poetry.

LEGAL DISCLAIMER: The views presented are those of the author and do not necessarily represent the views of the Department of Defense or its components.

Made in United States
Orlando, FL
22 June 2024